Navigating Bullying

Empowering Parents and Protecting Children

from Harm

Ivline I. Telfort

Table of Contents

What to Do If the Bullying Doesn't Stop?

Sadly, sometimes it's hard to get the bullying to stop. Some school districts aren't very good at stopping it, often due to funding issues. And sometimes a bully lives in the neighborhood, and the bullying happens after school. In that case, you have to deal with the parents directly, and that can be even more difficult than dealing with a school.

Here are some tips on what to do if the bullying won't stop.

* Contact the Teacher – If bullying happens at school, always contact your child's teacher directly first. Don't ever contact the parents in this case because it's better for you and your child if the school deals with the issue instead of you. This can help defuse a situation and avoid

more problems if the parents don't act appropriately due to their child being a bully.

* Contact the Parents – If the bullying is happening in your neighborhood and not at school, you may need to notify the parents. The best thing to do is to try a calm approach at first. If you can get proof of the bullying behavior to show the parents, that will help. It's not easy to hear that your child is doing something like this and today's parents often will not listen to you. But it's worth a try. Do stay calm and if they don't respond appropriately, let them know you will go to the police or get a lawyer.

* Contact the PTA – If the teacher isn't doing anything, contact the PTA and try to head up some anti-bullying training for the entire school. Often this way will work best for everyone. It doesn't single out either your child or the bully. Instead, it provides information, education, and solutions to everyone to help curb bullying for everyone.

* Contact the School Board – If that doesn't work, you may need to contact the school board to compel teachers to act and principals to provide the anti-bullying training

district-wide. This is a little harder to do but you have a right to attend these meetings and make it an issue.

* Contact a Lawyer – If all that fails, get a lawyer. You may be able to sue the school or the bully's parents to force them to get the bully some help to stop the bullying. This may cause a lot of turmoil for your child, though, so think hard before you go in this direction.

* Contact the Press – In a particularly egregious case, you may want to talk to the press about the situation so that the district or parent is forced to do something about the bully. Sometimes just the fear of exposure will get things done.

* Call the Police – If the bullying is in any way violent, racist, or involves some form of discrimination that is prosecutable, call the police. Often that can get things moving in the right direction quickly when nothing else works.

* Protect Your Child – While you're working to get things done and make a change, don't force your child to be around the bully. It's not fair that your child may have to stop going to school or may not be able to play outside in your neighborhood if the bully is nearby. But, the most

important thing is to protect your child and let them know they're loved and you don't blame them.

* Get Counseling for Your Child – Many children who are bullied ruthlessly are at a higher risk of committing suicide, drug use, and other problems. Get help for your child; even when you cannot stop the bullying (or help the bully), put your child's needs first and get counseling for them to help them improve their self-esteem.

Bullying can be very serious. Children have committed suicide due to the unbearable abuse that they put up with at the hands of a bully. Do whatever you can to remove your child from the situation, including homeschooling if you must. Don't force your child to have to live with the bullying if you can't get it to stop by any method.

What to Do If You Suspect Bullying but Aren't Sure?

Sometimes you get a feeling your child is being bullied but you have no proof because your child will not speak about it. Your child is showing signs that there is a problem; this could be through depression, illness, not wanting to go to school, and even displaying anger and bullying behavior to your other children. What can you do if you think it's happening but cannot get confirmation?

* Proceed as If You're Right – You don't need to know who is doing the bullying to move forward as if it's happening. Talk to the teacher and ask them to notice your child and what's happening due to your concern about their behavior, moods, or grades. Ask them directly if they notice any type of bullying going on, without asking them who. Teachers may not be allowed to tell you that

information anyway. Ask them about your child's behavior and what's happening to your child, not anyone else's.

* Bring It Up at the Next PTA Meeting – Your PTA organization can help with anti-bullying training for parents and the children at the school too. If you dedicate some funding toward an anti-bullying program and get all parents involved, you may be able to stop the bullying without ever knowing why, when, or who. Even if you're not sure whether your child is being bullied or not, someone's kid is being bullied if there is no program. You can count on having a program being of assistance to stop it. But, you may be the one who has to start it.

* Get Counseling for Your Child – If your child is acting out in a way that is dangerous to themselves and bad for their life and future (especially if you're worried about suicide), the best choice is always to get some extra help in the form of counseling. The best counselor probably isn't the one at school. Call your insurance company to get a good recommendation for counseling in your area.

* Spend Extra Time with Your Child – Anytime your child is not behaving properly or seems sad, depressed,

anxious, or is having a problem that you cannot figure out, the best way to deal with it is to spend more time with them. The more time you spend with them in a non-judgmental way, the more they may start opening up to you.

* Teach Your Child Self-Confidence – One thing that makes a child especially tempting for bullies to pick on is their level of self-confidence. A self-confident child will stand up for themselves, even when scared, and will tell on the bully. Bullies don't want to be told about. Bullies want the make the child cry, scared, and uncomfortable – if they end up in the uncomfortable position instead, they're not going to continue.

* Consider Homeschooling If Possible – If your child is especially unhappy with school, it could be bullying but it could be another problem. Not all kids do well in large classes with lots of people around. Some kids need homeschooling, a private school, smaller classes, or something else to thrive. Consider all the possibilities if your child is unhappy.

It's not fair when a child must put up with bullying. But, you don't even need to know who is doing it or what is happening to make a change for your child. Listen to your child about the other things they need. For example, if your child hates school and it's affecting their will to live, consider making a serious change for them to help them even if you're not sure why. They'll feel listened to and loved, and it will make a difference.

Do's and Don'ts When You Think Your Child Is Being Bullied

Bullying has been in the news a lot lately due to the advent of school shootings. The truth is there is no evidence that school shootings are being done by bullies. But, it is starting the conversation to encourage teachers, students, and parents to deal with the bullying problem rampant in schools and society today.

Don't Blame Your Child

This may seem like a no-brainer, but you'd be shocked to learn that there are people out there who blame the victim for being bullied. They'll claim with no facts to back it up that the child must be doing something to cause the other kids to bully them. But, usually, this is not the case at all. And if it was true, wouldn't bullies get bullied?

Instead, make sure that you tell your child that they aren't to blame and that it's not their fault. It's never the victim's fault about what happens to them. Bullies choose any convenient target to attack and tend to keep picking on victims that react in a way that they like, but that doesn't make it the victim's fault.

Don't Joke About It

Some parents and siblings think that it's best to make light of the situation, but the truth is it's one of the worst things that you can do. For a child who is being bullied, their life becomes a horrible ordeal that they must get through whenever they are just doing the normal things they need to do each day, like going to school.

Instead, take the child seriously and let them know that you take it seriously. Comfort them and encourage them to realize that if others are teasing them, it's not something you think is funny or that anyone should think is funny.

Don't Immediately Blame the School

While it would be nice if class sizes were smaller, the truth is most educators have no choice but to try to control and teach 30 kids in a class (and even more in some places). This makes it hard to notice everything that is happening. That's not an excuse; it's the reality of where we are with education, at least in the USA.

What you can do instead is talk to the teacher, the principal, and other interested parties and try to craft a plan to address the problem in a way that helps your child. The main thing is to show everyone that the bullied child is supported and that bullying will not be tolerated in your school.

Don't Hide the Situation

Even if your child is embarrassed by the situation, don't hide it from the school or anyone. If it's open knowledge that a certain child is bullying your child, even other kids will start to realize that this is not a good thing, and the bully may stop just due to positive peer pressure. This openness is going to help remove the shame of the situation from the bullied child.

Don't Encourage Violence

It seems like a good movie plot. The bullied child strikes back and beats up the bully. Or the best friend beats up the bully. Someone always beats up the bully. But the truth is, violence is just making the problem worse. If you react in a better way, you're going to be more likely to stop the bullying behavior long-term.

While you don't want your child to be a doormat, you do want them to find other ways to deal with issues than violence when it is possible. Of course, if the bully starts hitting your child, your child should feel that they have full permission to defend themselves.

Don't Ignore the Problem

Many parents think that if they just ignore the problem, it'll eventually go away. Unfortunately, if a bully is getting a response from your child, they may never stop until both are out of school unless you figure out how to stop it.

When you talk about the problem in the open, it's going to be easier to solve. As a parent, you can't ignore the problem because you're responsible for your child emotionally and physically. Ignoring the issue may encourage even more bullying.

Don't Criticize Your Child

It is true that often a bully picks a certain child due to their reaction to the abuse. They easily push the child's buttons, making them cry or get scared. The bully loves this type of interaction as it makes them feel powerful. But your child meanwhile feels powerless and likely suffers from some PTSD, which will enhance their reactions even more.

Instead, encourage higher self-esteem in your child so that they can resist reacting to the bully more effectively. Plus, encourage them to tell a teacher, find a buddy, and report to you anything that happens each day.

Don't Contact the Bully's Parents

It might be tempting to call the bully's parents and tell on the child. But the problem is that most parents don't welcome this type of call and react poorly to it. You may even cause more problems for your child than they already have.

Instead, tell the school administration and let them know that you expect some form of action on the bullying to include school-wide anti-bullying training for teachers, students, and parents. The bullying training can occur on a PTA meeting night so that parents know how to recognize signs that their child is being abused or that their child is being abused.

Don't Let Anger Guide You

When your child is being harmed, it's easy to get angry. This is most especially true when a child is being bullied and you feel as if the school and administration (or the other parents) aren't doing enough to stop it.

Instead of getting angry, start educating people. Offer to lead a program at the school to stop bullying. You can get these materials from various organizations including Stop Bullying Now. (http://stopbullyingnow.com/)

Using this guide is going to make it easier to deal with a situation of bullying. If you think your child is being bullied, don't delay getting everyone involved to put a stop to it.

How to Get Support from the School

When your child is being bullied at school, the school needs to be involved in detection, consequences to the bully, and prevention. Without the school helping with this, there is no way to stop the bullying without removing your child from school entirely. Learning how to get support from the school can help end bullying for your child and all children after.

* Teach Your Child How to Stand Up for Themselves – The very first thing you must do when your child reports to you that they're being bullied is to teach them the way to stand up for themselves that works best for them without worrying about getting into trouble. Nothing they're doing is causing the abuse, but being aware of their body language, raising their self-image, and giving

them permission to tell on the bully or respond to the bully, can go far in helping curb bullying.

* Make an Appointment with Your Child's Teacher – Now you want to make an appointment with your child's teacher. This appointment should include you, your child (sometimes), and school counselors and administrators but not the child doing the bullying or their parents. It's best if the school deals separately with them to protect your child from retribution.

* Bring Anti-Bullying Education with You – Sometimes due to a lack of resources, school officials don't have information about bullying at their fingertips. You can download information about bullying from various online sites, including anti-bullying sites created by the federal government.

* Stay Calm and Positive – Don't go to the meeting angry and start yelling at people. While it's tempting to do that when your child is being hurt, it's not the best way to get the right response from educators. In fact, they may start seeing you as a problem and not help at all. That isn't a good thing so when you are talking to them, stay calm.

It's also important to stay calm and positive in front of your child.

* Be Persistent – It can sometimes be difficult to get the school to do anything about the bullying due to lack of time and funds. But, if you're persistent and they know you're going to follow up on everything they promise, they're going to be more likely to stick to it and make the situation better.

* Contact the Superintendent – If the administration of your school isn't doing enough after trying for some time (and keeping track of what you do), contact the superintendent and ask them to intervene. This usually is enough to get the laziest administration to do something.

* Contact the Law – If your child is in danger and has been physically attacked or threatened and calls to the school have only resulted in making it worse, or nothing getting better, report it to the police. Sometimes it can help to contact a lawyer to send a letter to the school but the police, if called, must do an investigation which is more than likely your school system doesn't want to happen.

* Start an Anti-Bullying Program via Your Parent-Teacher Organization – Schools are notoriously low in funds, and

staff. It can be hard for them to do a good anti-bullying program. But, with the help of your teacher organization and you, the school may happily allow you to take over that job which can do wonders for all the kids at your school.

Getting support from the school to deal with bullying is essential to stopping it. If you don't get that support, it can be hard or even impossible to really make a change. Don't give up, though, and don't let anger drive you. Let the desire to stop bullying for your child and others guide you by making you an example of anti-bullying.

Online Resources to Help You and Your Child

Finding bullying resources is simple today with the advent of the internet. Online anti-bullying information is everyplace. It's important to differentiate between good information and poor information, though. Good information seeks to prevent bullying without ever blaming the child for being bullied. The following sites offer accurate information that you can easily access from the comfort of your home or the classroom.

* StopBullying.gov – This is a US Government site that has a lot of information about combatting bullying and educating the public about bullying. You can teach both the bullied and bullies about why bullying is bad and how to stop it. They are in partnership with the Department of Education and provide up-to-date information to help stop bullying.

* NoBullying.com – This website claims to be the "World's Authority" on bullying and it's true they have tons of information about how to help different groups of people regarding bullying. They have a lot of stats that you can gather to help you educate others. For example, did you know that 43 percent of kids report that they've been a victim of online bullying?

* Anti-Bullying Alliance – This organization is out of London, England. They have so much information and it's laid out very well. Even if you're in another place, you can use a lot of the tips. They have a lot of advice for everyone, including teachers, students, parents, and others. You can even find a program that you can start in your local school with support.

Link - https://www.anti-bullyingalliance.org.uk/

* ActAgainstViolence.apa.org – This organization is from Washington DC and they have a lot of information about bullying as well as other issues. You can get handouts, tip sheets, webinars, and more, all about preventing violence and raising safe kids, and creating strong families. The goal is to stop violence in our families and in our schools.

* American Academy of Child & Adolescent Psychiatry – This is a great place to find bullying facts and information as well as guides to help families combat bullying, whether their child is being bullied or is the bully. Often a child who has been bullied needs help to build self-esteem, and finding a counselor for them can help. Likewise, if you have a child who is a bully, getting professional help for them can make all the difference.

Link - https://www.aacap.org/aacap/Families_and_Youth/Resource_Centers/Bullying_Resource_Center/Home.aspx

* Child Safety Network – This organization (which is part of the Education Development Center in Massachusetts) has a great bullying prevention resource guide that you can use, as well as toolkits, programs, campaigns, and more. Plus, you can find even more organizations that may help you overcome a bullying situation with your child.

Link - https://www.edc.org/sites/default/files/uploads/BullyingPrevention.pdf

Bullying is a chronic problem in most schools and should be addressed prior to any problems being developed. Schools that start an anti-bullying program from day one are less likely to have serious bullying problems.

Eight Signs That a Younger Child Is Being Bullied

Sometimes children don't tell us everything that goes on in their lives - even when they're in elementary school. But, there are signs you can watch out for in case your child is being bullied. It's important to be aware of your child, their moods, and their physical condition at all times, and this will give you a good guide to help you keep your child safe.

Here are some signs that may indicate that your child is being bullied.

1. They Don't Want to Go to School – If your child always loved school and then suddenly doesn't like it and makes excuses not to go, it is a sign that something is wrong. It

might be bullying but it could also be something else. The best thing to do is to ask the child what is wrong.

2. They Revert to Infantile Behavior – If your younger child seems super-stressed out and starts acting infantile again, especially before or after school, that could be a sign that something not right is happening to them at school. Examples of this behavior include thumb-sucking, potty accidents, bedwetting, and a lot of crying.

3. They Are Always Sick to Their Stomachs or Complain of Headaches – If your child is getting more stomach issues and headaches, try to figure out what is causing them. For example, if it's after school or before school, are they overtired, or is something happening at the school that you need to investigate?

4. Your Child Has Changed Friend Groups Recently – If your child up until recently always had the same friends and now suddenly they don't have the same friends, it's worth investigating. What happened? What caused the change? Sometimes children actually hang out with the child that is bullying them and pressuring them to do things they don't like - especially if they're younger, shy, and socially inexperienced.

5. They're Having Trouble Sleeping – If your younger child is suddenly having trouble sleeping, waking up with nightmares, and having other sleep issues, you might want to find out what's happening at school. Often emotional problems can manifest during times that should be relaxing.

6. They Are Having Panic Attacks – If your child suddenly starts having panic attacks before school or at school, you may want to determine if something is happening at school that can be stopped, such as bullying.

7. They Withdraw from the Family – Sometimes a young child will actually withdraw from the people they're most safe with due to bullying at school or on the playground. The reason has to do with the fact that they may feel ashamed even though it's not their fault.

8. They Have Torn Clothing or Marks – Sometimes bullying is more than mental. It can also be physical, even at very young ages. If your child has torn clothing, marks such as bite marks, bruises, and other signs of a struggle, bullying may be occurring.

When you notice that your child has any of these signs, don't let them avoid talking to you. Instead, give them the freedom to talk to you by letting them feel safe. After all, if your child feels safe and not judged as if they're in trouble when you react to their situation, they're going to be much more likely to talk to you about whatever is happening to them.

The Different Types of Bullying

Bullying comes in seven different forms that can easily be recognizable. Often a bully will use more than one type of bullying to really cause chaos in their victim's life. The best way to deal with any type of bullying is directly - by ending the ability for the bully to have access to their victim, then giving everyone education about it.

1. Physical - This type of bullying is also physical abuse. This happens when the bully punches, bites, and otherwise makes physical threats against the person they are bullying, to intimate them. They may also take the lunch money, toys, and books, and destroy the property of their target. This type of bullying is the most immediately dangerous due to the risk of injury and even death, and most of the time it requires the law to get involved.

2.   Verbal – Sometimes physical bullying also has a component of verbal abuse simultaneously. This type of bullying includes persistent name-calling, threats, and other verbal abuse that ruins the self-esteem of the victim.

3. Emotional – This type of bullying can be very pervasive and often happens within peer groups as well as relationships. For example, a boyfriend or girlfriend might withhold love if the person isn't acting how they want them to in a way that is abusive.

4. Sexual – Any type of unwanted physical, verbal, or emotional contact that is sexual in nature and repetitive is a form of sexual bullying. For example, a young girl might get made fun of on a bus because her breasts are bouncing during the ride to school or home, causing her a lot of shame.

5. Racist – This type of bullying may be made through jokes, slurs, racist posters, and even physical intimation using known racist symbols, terms, and gestures. A person using racist bullying may make fun of the victim's way of dressing, praying, or living according to their culture.

6. Social – This often happens in peer groups where a group bullies a victim into doing things they really didn't want to do such as use drugs, perform sexual acts, or do other things - even how they dress. It can be mild or very dangerous.

7. Cyber – This is any type of bullying that happens through online means such as chats, social media, instant messaging, texting, recording, or doing other things to embarrass or target the victim in question.

These seven types of bullying are all too common. If you can determine the type of bullying, you may also be able to find the key to making the bullying stop by controlling the environment of the ones who bully as well as the ones being bullied. You can provide more supervision, more controls, as well as education for everyone to stop it.

Tips for Getting Your Child to Tell You About It

The best defense against bullying is openness and talking about it. But it can often be hard to get your child to do that. They may be ashamed, embarrassed, or scared that you'll have a "bad" reaction. You can help mitigate this issue by not showing your emotions and being clinical about the discussion so that you can get your child to talk to you.

1. Don't Be Emotional – Keep your emotions to yourself. If you get too sad, angry, or emotional when talking to your child about any issue, they're going to back off the discussion. Your emotions are very important to them and can overwhelm the strongest child. Try to show concern without tears, shaky voice, or other problems that can signal to your child that you're distressed.

2. Ask Your Child Open-Ended Questions – When you ask your child questions about bullying, it's best to ask questions that require more than a "yes or no" answer. If you don't do that they'll just say yes or no, and you won't get the information you want and need from them.

3. Do Not Judge Your Child – No matter what your child tells you, don't judge them or make them feel judged. That's not the best way to get them to tell you things. Even if they reacted badly to the situation, it's not the time to judge. Instead, it's the time to listen to them so that you know what to do next.

4. Notice the Signs – Learn the signs of bullying so that you can pay attention to what is going on without even talking to your child. That way you have a clue about what questions to ask your child when you do try to talk to them about bullying.

5. Avoid the Word "Bully" – It's best not to use the word "bully" when you're talking to them about bullying. Instead, talk about the behaviors when you're identifying what happened to them. For example, if your child talks about someone at school who is physically intimidating

them, don't call that child a bully - just talk about the behavior.

6. Help Them Build Anti-Bullying Skills – Do talk to your child about how to mitigate bullying by not responding in the way that the child doing the mean behavior likes. For example, many bullies act that way to intimidate someone who they see as competition. If you want to stop them, don't respond in a way that shows them it's working.

7. Understand the Causes of Bullying – If you can get into the research about the types of things that causes a child to participate in bullying, you can also usually figure out how to stop it. Many bullies are simply scared kids who are trying to get control. That doesn't help your child who is being harmed right away, but you can possibly put a stop to the bullying by understanding the behavior long term.

8. Listen – The best thing you can do to get your child to talk to you is to listen to them. When you listen, you'll repeat what you think you heard, and you'll also not judge, nor try to tell them what to do right away or overreact to anything.

When talking about anything with your child, including bullying, it's imperative that you don't let your emotions take over. It will make your child clam up and be afraid to go further into the discussion. Keep your calm and let them talk more than you. You'll get much more information that way.

ARC Bullying – Tweets

Do's and Don'ts When You Think Your Child Is Being Bullied

Tweet: Do's and don'ts if your child is being bullied. LINK

How to Get Support from the School

Tweet: How to get support from the school if your child is being bullied. LINK

Online Resources to Help You and Your Child

Tweet: Helpful online resources if your child is being bullied. LINK

Eight Signs That a Younger Child Is Being Bullied

Tweet: These 8 signs can mean that your younger child is being bullied. LINK

Eight Signs That an Older Child Is Being Bullied

Tweet: 8 signs that can mean that your older child is being bullied. LINK

The Different Types of Bullying

Tweet: 7 different types of bullying. LINK

Tips for Getting Your Child to Tell You About It

Tweet: Do you suspect that your child is being bullied? Here are 8 ways to get them to talk about it. LINK

What Makes a Child Become a Target for Bullying?

Tweet: What makes a child become a target for bullies? Learn more here. LINK

What to Do If the Bullying Doesn't Stop?

Tweet: Advice on what to do if your child is being bullied and it won't stop. LINK

What to Do If You Suspect Bullying but Aren't Sure?

Tweet: Is your child being bullied? Here's what to do if you suspect but aren't sure. LINK

What Makes a Child Become a Target for Bullying?

While most parents want a list of the things that can cause a child to become a target for bullying, understand that this list is just a norm. It's not the definitive rule. Plus, there are always exceptions depending on what type of school it is, what's considered normal in that culture or community, and how the school administration and community deal with issues surrounding bullying.

* The Teacher's Pet – Often a teacher's pet is a target, mostly because they are good at something. Usually, they're super-smart kids who want to get A's and like getting the teacher's attention and succeed in doing so. The other kids feel as if the pet is being treated better than them and they start trying to put the child in their place.

* Creative Types – Sometimes creative children like to dress differently, act a little differently and stand out. In schools without anti-bullying training, that child may end up being made fun of due to their clothing or actions that aren't the norm in that community. This type of shaming happens to try to force the child to act like everyone else.

* Introverted Children – Some children don't really want to be friends with a bunch of other kids and prefer to sit alone and are fine with it. However, this can make the child a target because most kids just want to belong, and it makes the other kids feel attacked for their desire to be with others even though nothing like that is happening.

* Anxious Children – Some kids just get super nervous around anyone that talks to them. They are anxious, and sometimes they're depressed, sad, or have other conditions that make them stand out in a way that other kids find odd. Then other kids pick on the anxious child to get a reaction out of them.

* Submissive Children – Some people are naturally more submissive than others and don't naturally try to defend themselves. They may be smaller than other kids and

scared to death. They may cry. They may make a scene that excites the bully to bully them even more.

* Children Who Don't Make Friends Easily – Some children have a hard time making friends, and are very awkward socially even though they don't want to be. This type of difference is taken as the child being stuck up or thinking they're better than the other kids, which then causes the kids to start bullying that child.

* Children Who Are Different – Any type of difference from normative standards will make a child a target. Whether it's bright red hair, sexuality, or something else that makes the child stand out as different, it can be a whistle call to the bullies to attack.

* Children Who Make the Bully Feel Threatened – Sometimes bullying happens because the bully feels threatened. The bully might be a leader in the school and gets all the other kids to attack that child they feel threatened by. It happens within sports teams, academic teams, and any type of competitive group.

* Children Who Have Unique Physical Characteristics – Some children may have characteristics that make them stand out. For example, they may have lots of freckles,

warts, or something on them that makes them stand out as not normal to the bullies, making them a target.

* Children Who Have an Illness or Disability – Sadly, children who are sick or disabled often get picked on too. Bullying can be extremely bad in these cases, as often these children are totally unable to defend themselves on their own.

* Children Who Have an Uncommon Religion – Often, children who have extreme religions that control how they dress, wear their hair, and act, so that they stand out and seem very different, end up being bullied. Jewish, Muslim, Fundamentalists, Polygamists, and so forth are in danger of being bullied more often than most.

* Children Who Are in the Minority Race – When a child's race stands out as different in the community, they may be subject to violent racial bullying that can harm them mentally and physically.

Even though these things can make children targets, this in no way implies that it's their fault. It's not. Children have to be taught that it's okay to be different and it's wrong to pick on people because of their differences or even if they have an annoying personality. It's never okay to pick on anyone for any reason whatsoever.